IT DOES NOT SAY MEOW

and other animal riddle rhymes

it does not

Clarion Books
a Houghton Mifflin Company imprint
215 Park Avenue South, New York, NY 10003
Text copyright © 1972 by Beatrice Schenk de Regniers
Illustrations copyright © 1972 by Paul Galdone
Library of Congress Catalog Card Number: 72-75704
ISBN: 0-395-28822-3
Printed in the USA
(Previously published by The Seabury Press
under ISBN: 0-8164-3086-1.)
HOR 10

say
meow

and other
animal riddle rhymes

BEATRICE SCHENK DE REGNIERS

Pictures by PAUL GALDONE

CLARION BOOKS
NEW YORK

It has a tail
For chasing flies.
It says *Mm-oo*
And looks at you
With big brown eyes.

It gives you milk
If you know how
To take it. Yes —
It is a...

COW

Soft paws.
Sharp claws.
Thick fur.
Loud purr.
What is that?
Yes! A...

cat

It has two feet,
No hands, two wings.
It can fly
In the sky.

Sometimes it chirps.
Sometimes it sings
The sweetest song
You ever heard.
Can you guess?
It is a...

bird

A short short tail.
A long long nose
He uses for
A water hose.

Two great big ears.
Four great big feet.
A tiny peanut
Is a treat
                for him.

His name is El —
Oh no! I can't!
Now *you* tell *me:*
An...

elephant

Six legs for walking.
Mouth for eating — not talking.
Does not make a sound.
Sleeps under the ground.
Likes picnics, but can't
Bring its own. It's an …

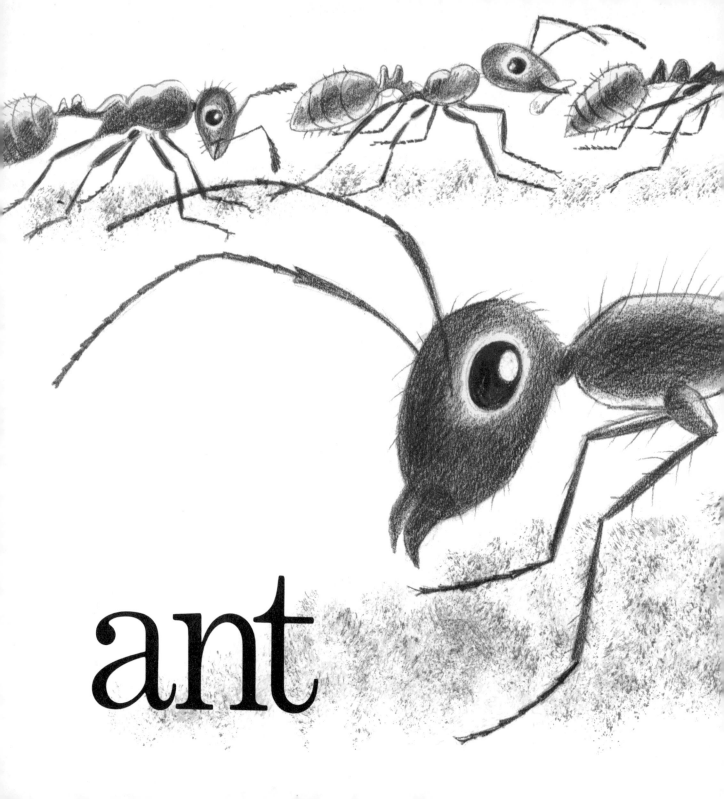

ant

A tail, thin and long.
Teeth sharp and strong.

It nibbles and gnaws.
Has four tiny paws,

Eyes beady bright,
Fur smooth and white.

Two can stand
Upon my hand.
I think they're nice.
What are they? …

mice

When it is born
It is all head and tail
        —mostly tail.
You could keep it at home
In a tub or a pail
        —a very small pail.

When it's grown up
It has no more tail.
Hoppity hop,
It jumps out of the pail.

Now it swims in a pond
Or hops on dry land.
Catches flies with its tongue
And sings a loud song,
Ka-ga-lunk or *Ka-chug*,
As it sits on a log.
It's a . . .

frog

It's glad when you're glad,
Sad when you're sad,
Has a head you can pat,
But it is not a cat.
(It does *not* say *me-ow*.)
And it doesn't say *moo*,
So it is not a cow.
It says *woof* or *bow-wow*.
Does that sound like a frog?
No! It's a…

dog

It's busy as a bee.
It's buzzy as a bee.
Looks funny as a bee.
Makes honey like a bee.

It must be a...

bee

Penny for a penny.
Stone for a stone.
Do you want more riddles? ..

Make up your own!